Before You Know It

Also by S.K. Williams
*Love by Night*
*Maybe Today*

# Before You Know It

S.K. Williams

Andrews McMeel
PUBLISHING®

*For the young versions of us.*
*Your courage, curiosity, and uncertainty*
*led us to who we are today.*

*Thank you*
*for being so brave.*

# Charting the Course

# Prologue

Have you ever looked around a crowded room and thought about how complex each and every single person's life is? What struggles are they going through? What makes them laugh? Who do they think of when they hear the word "love"?

Kevin and I wanted to write a book about the time period between eighteen and twenty-eight. The first decade of adult life – the decade that is coming to an end for us. Let me tell you something you already know. Growing up is tough. There's no one right way to do it, and no matter how much guidance you might have, you'll still make some mistakes along the way.

The hard part for us – because this was the most difficult book we've written so far – was writing our experiences in a way that felt relatable. We made very different life choices – and we couldn't always relate to each other.

In my twenties, I struggled in an unhealthy marriage and divorce before meeting Kevin. With weight gain and loss, with agoraphobia, loneliness, and paralyzing fear. But I also flourished in my self-growth, relationships, careers, and outlook on the world and myself.

In Kevin's twenties, he struggled living the (literally) starving artist life in Los Angeles. With crushing debt, an unhealthy relationship, living paycheck to paycheck, powerlessness, and never being enough. But he also flourished in his self-growth, taking control, setting boundaries, and realizing that things work out in the end, just not always as you planned.

Our hope is that between the two of us, you might be able to find some friends who have been through what you might be going through right now. Each chapter has two parts – one from my perspective and one from Kevin's. The book progresses from eighteen at the start to twenty-eight by the end.

If you're at the start of your adulthood journey, we hope to give you the knowledge that you won't be alone. If you're in the middle, you can already see some of the growth you've achieved, and you know there will be more to come. And if you're at the end, nearing thirty like us, you know the journey never really ends. This is a voyage everyone sails, no matter how different our paths may be.

We hope this book gives you comfort. We hope it provides you with friendship, encouragement, and understanding in the bad and good times. And before you know it, life can be pretty amazing.

– Shayla

# In The Beginning

# PART ONE

For the first time in my life,
I'm being told how much potential I have
People I respect and look up to
think *I'm* capable

It feels like flying – or maybe falling –
this trepidatious self-confidence
It feels like for the first time
maybe, just maybe,
I can trust myself to live my best life

I want to make them proud of me
and maybe in striving for that
I'll learn to be proud of myself too

When the sunset is pink and dreamy,
and the windows are rolled down
as we speed over the looming hill
to get that roller-coaster rush
down in the pit of our stomachs,

When we stay up late and binge eat
ice cream and melting mozzarella sticks,
talking about everything and nothing
all at once,

When the songs we blast can't be loud enough
as we belt out lyrics
we don't even pay attention to,

When I come over and just sit with you
because your depression is hard today,

And I think how long it's been since
I've had this with anyone . . .

I'm so glad I have a best friend like you.

If you act in a situation
in such a way
that you can sleep at night
and feel good about how you handled yourself,

Then *that's* what truly matters.

Things may not always work out
the way you want them to.
You can't make everyone happy –
no matter how hard you try.

If you feel you did your best,

Then you did well
and I am proud of you.

*– Advice from my father*

In this new place
I blend in almost like a ghost
trying so hard to not be seen
I think – I *hope* –
that most of the time I succeed.

But I know I wear my emotions on my sleeve
and I'm so sure sometimes that everyone sees
how small
how scared
how pitiful I am.

Some days, I just want to disappear.

I feel like I'm caught in a whirlpool
spinning around and around
dizzied by everything expected of me

How do I swim out
when I'm nauseous from going in the
same circles

Who said I had to be here?
Who is churning this life?

Because it isn't me
and I want no part of it

### Big Ideas

I want to be a beach bum –
have a little shack on the California coast
with friends who are
as easygoing as I want to be.

I want to spend all my days by the salty ocean,
my skin warm and brown,
my hair kissed by the sun.
I know I'll be happy there.

I'll make it by with odd jobs –
I won't need much
because it'll be a simple life
and I know I'll be happy there.

I'll live like Gidget or Frankie Avalon
and have beach parties
and surf the curling waves
all day long
and I *know* I'll be happy there.

*Won't I?*

I'll keep on walking
like so many of my ancestors before me
but I don't know where I'm going
and I'm not sure what I'm doing.

I'm losing the faith I had in myself –
the promise that I felt instilled in me
has grown stale
after almost no time at all.

It was so easy to lose.

Maybe I'm not cut out for this life.

But all I can do is keep walking
because even though it feels fruitless
it's the only thing I know how to do.

Where do you find the strength
to be who you want to be?

I wonder who else
stepped these same roads
before me.

## Am I Brave Enough? (Part I)

At eighteen, I had this date
with a guy I met online who
was six years older than me.

We met at the grocery store
and I wanted out as soon as I saw him
riding a BMX bike
with a foxtail clipped to his back beltloop.
But I didn't say anything.

We walked around town, and he wanted to
go by his house to drop off his bike before
we went to a trail I'd never been to.
I was nervous he'd ask me inside
but he just dumped his bike in the driveway
like a kid.

We talked about everything he wanted.
I barely said a word, I hardly needed to.
I wondered how long this would last,
but I didn't say anything.

It was summer and sweltering out.
On the trail with minimal people
I peeled off my jacket and after a while, we sat.

He raised his arm and with his index finger
traced along the outline of my bra
*I can see your bra line . . .*
*Does this bother you?*

It did. Very much.
But no one was in sight
and I didn't know what to do.

I thought of two options:

Either say *yes* but risk coming off
weak – easy target –
or say *no* in a confident but dissuading voice
and put my jacket back on –
he'd leave me alone then, right?

I opted for number two.
I don't know why.
It doesn't make sense to me now.

He texted me incessantly after that date,
even after I said
I wasn't looking for a relationship.

I blocked him and never heard from him again.
But it always bothered me that
I didn't say anything.

And I ask myself,
*Would I be brave enough*
*to speak up if this happened again?*

It scares me that I don't know the answer.

People always compare freedom
to a bird flying,
untethered and weightless,
reckless and fearless,
doing whatever the hell they want
while riding the thermals.

But no one ever talks about freedom
being like a turtle,
crawling on slowly in your growth,
going at your own pace,
creating a safe space inside yourself
where you can be utterly and entirely at peace.

## Sock

I am a lone sock
not part of a pair or a pack
or maybe I was
but now they've all gone.

I sit alone in a drawer
around happy others and think
where I might have been able to go
if I didn't lose such a necessary part of me.

Little did I realize how desperate
I would feel to not be alone
and I wonder what I would do –
how far I would go –
for this to not be so.

## Bird Cage

I am small —
the size of a finch
inside a massive cage
huddled up in the center,
        knees hugged up to my chest.

All around me is quiet blackness,
the shadows like tentacles reaching
inside to grasp me;
the darkness is suffocating.

It keeps me here,
confined,
        where I should be.
        It reminds me that I don't belong,
        that I'm not wanted,
        not worth the space.

So, I stay quiet,
        stay small,
        stay out of sight.

### Schrödinger's Future

To be new
in a place,
to a person,
is like ice water on a hot day.

It's just what you need to
stop the stagnation
or at least distract from it.

With potential renewed,
fresh life breathed into you,
anything can happen again.

I *hope* it works.

Alone doesn't always mean lonely
and it isn't always bad
but it is always
obvious

Lonely doesn't always mean alone
sometimes it's a throbbing ache
other times it sneaks
up on you

— *I didn't even realize*

There is nothing quite like
a university campus
with ancient brick buildings
overlooking dewy green grass
dappled with students.

Their windows look at you with
knowledge you'll never acquire
in this lifetime.

And it feels as though they can
see directly into your soul
in the most comforting of ways.

Like a seedling growing
stronger every day,
I am feeling myself becoming
more than I was yesterday.

Knowledge is more than facts and dates,
numbers and books,
theories and subjects.

Knowledge is a faction of existence
that feeds our souls,
informs our instincts,
and brings us closer to something
we may never understand in this life.

Don't take it for granted.

Sometimes the path is made of
quicksand and you haven't
even realized
until you're drowning.

The panic attacks happen at night
always keeping me up to early morning
without reprieve
and I cannot stop it.
 I cannot stop it.

Each day it gets harder to wake up,
more terrifying to go outside.

The worst parts of me are taking over
like a heavy blanket of kudzu –
a burden to myself and others.
And all I can do is cry

Sit in the dark closet
until I'm coaxed to crawl out.

No one ever knew the amount of strength
I needed to open that door.

I thought I'd keep some friends as I grew older
or at least make some new ones

But I find that I don't have anyone to turn to
no one to call or spend time with

I see others with their groups
and I can't help but feel the sting
of jealousy

Maybe if I weren't so shy
maybe if I were different

Maybe there's something wrong with me

Cottonwood is a thick smell
that sits in your lungs and fills up your throat.
I've never decided if I like it or not.

It makes it snow in spring,
and never trust that there isn't a caterpillar nest
in the branches – because there always is.

Cotton has a way of getting everywhere
outside and inside you.

But I always feel peaceful when it blooms.

It permeates warmth, freedom, contentedness.
The heavy smell demands your attention,
commanding you to be mindful of
your surroundings, to breathe, relax,
slow down.

To take no chances,
to play it easy,
to be as safe as possible,

It's a life led by fear.
A life led by distrust of oneself,
always doubting your own capacity
and capabilities.

It's a life led by constricting a cage
around your heart and not letting
it pump the way it needs to fully feel.

To tell yourself *no* every time an adventure
presents itself
because you grew up being told
you aren't worth the time.

I wish I could be different.

PART TWO

### Eighteen

When the molting snakeskin falls away,
which pieces of me will stay?

When you pretend to be someone else
for too long,
sometimes you forget
who you were before.

I never let them see the real me
hiding underneath,
heavy eyes from sleepless nights,
focused on some college-ruled page,
writing to escape the haze.

They don't know the real me,
and now that I think about it,
neither do I.

I just turned eighteen,
and I wonder now, if I can be anything,
who is it really
that I want to call *me?*

**Daydreams**

I've always been told what to do,

Where to go, what to say, every single day
and I never feel okay.

Whenever I can,
I stow pieces of myself away.

And when no one is watching,
I blot out the world around me
and drift off outside my body.

Rolling over starlit seas,
swimming across cloud-streaked skies,
carving through canyons,
all beckoning me
in scenes unfolding behind my eyes.

The heat of the sun
soaking into my skin,
the cawing of gulls in the distance,
all – longingly –
pulling me deeper in.

I want to stay here, in this place, so far away –
this world where I finally feel like I *belong*.

When I don't know where I am going,
I will look up to the stars,
I will listen to the wild *breath* of the wind,
I will lay my fingers upon the lapping waves,
and trust that the world will
know the way.

There are so many places to go,
doors anxiously waiting to be opened,
ready to be explored.

I find it hard
to think every single possibility through,
to know which door is right.

It's easier to stay here
than to commit, to see it through,
wherever I go,
whatever I decide to do.

Every choice has the potential
to be some big mistake
that I just don't want to make.

But every choice has potential
to be something *good*, too,
to make me happy
if only I can find the courage
to open the door and see.

### Caretaker

I've spent too many days
looking after those
who wrestle with themselves,
waiting for them to see
the better person they could be.

I thought
if I could lend a little light
to those stumbling through the dark,
they could find their way back home
to the truth lying deep in their heart.

But now I see the cost:
my own starry glow has begun to fade.

My days are swallowed up
and only the nights belong to me,
spent wandering the streets,
searching for my forgotten youth,
lost in lonely thoughts,
filling up journals.

When will the days come
when someone else takes care of *me?*

**Automaton**

I cannot help
who I am.

I will always do
whatever must be done.

I cannot pretend
the cycle will ever end.

Automaton, this is what I am.
How do I turn it off?
How do I make it stop?

No chance to be
anything different
than whatever they tell me to be,
than whatever they need from me.

Automaton, will it ever end?

Automaton, *turn it off.*

## Graduation

How do you say *goodbye*
to a place you've never really been?

I was a ghost wandering these halls.
I remember back to the first day
and that feeling I didn't belong, not even then.

At the end of my first day of freshman year,
I learned my father died.
I tucked him in a padded wooden box,
arms crossed over his chest for a final rest,
and when I came back – there was a heaviness
I pushed down deep inside myself,
a heavy roar compacted in,
a sweeping gale that lifted me up off my feet,
and I never touched these school grounds again.

I floated on, going through the motions,
each day, each class, wishing it were the last,
not knowing where I was – much less where
I would go when the raging storm had passed.
One foot stepping out the door,
eager to leave – to move forward, to find more,
knowing what was required of me,
knowing at last who I had to be.

When people say they had to grow up fast,
they don't often talk about the childhood
they left behind somewhere in the past,
the kid they never got to be.

How do I say goodbye,
except for *good riddance?*

People are incredibly durable things.
We get beaten up, torn down, and heartbroken

but we still find a way to get back up
and put ourselves back together.

Starry-eyed, hopeful, smiling wide,
and the most determined I had ever been,
I packed up everything I owned
into my sister's sky-blue sedan.

We drove the twenty-one hours
over two days' time
and arrived in Los Angeles,
prepared to start a new chapter,
to write some brand-new lines.

And as she braved back north alone,
I looked around me and took it all in.
This was the first day of a new beginning,
a new life where I would let myself *belong*
in a way that I had never been before.

*This is it,*
I remember thinking.
*This* is where you go
when you let yourself dream,
when you let yourself believe
you can be *anything*.

### Home

I don't know why,
but whenever I draw closer to the ocean,
it always feels like coming home.

There's nothing like the sight of
rays of soothing sunshine
breaking through the clouds,

The calming taste
in the spray of ocean mist
breathed in through sunbaked lips,

The tranquil feeling
in the warmth of soothing sand
slipping between wriggling toes,
massaging hardened heels and calloused hands.

These waves are a gentle reminder
that the world, like me, is very much alive.
I listen to her heartbeat
and lie down beside her,
my cheek laid down against the tender shore,
pulsing soft beneath the sunset.

I tell her I have come home
and she holds me in her hands,
maternal and pure.

## Mirror (Part I)

*Who are you?* they'll ask
because it's always a part of your first day.

*Who am I?* I wonder – staring in the mirror.

When did all this acne
burst to the surface?
Some cruel joke that waited my entire life
for the perfect punch line.

Four years and thirty-two products
and not one step closer to clear skin.

I thought I would outgrow this.

How can I expect them to look at me
and see past all this
when it's all that *I* can see?

Why is this happening to me?

## Opening Up

Do I have to let them in
if I want them to let *me* in?

Some scars stayed quiet so long,
they lie dormant gathering dust
and I don't know if they even remember
how to speak.

If I let it out and I tell them who I really am,
if I'm raw and I'm real,
What if it never stops unfolding?
What if I can't find a way to hide it –
to pack it all back inside?

I want to help everyone else
but I don't know if *I* can be better.

Does that even matter?
Do *I* even matter?
Or is it all for them – everyone else –
even this? This opening up.

You spend your nights awake,
You cover up your scars,
because you think your pain
is too much to take.

You hide yourself within,
but inside, you're already past your limit,
and it's starting to spill up over the brim.

Maybe you need to let a little out,
to make enough room to let someone else in.

Maybe you don't hear it enough,
but it's okay if all you can manage
is half a smile, a one-word response,
or tired eyes eager to say goodbye.

Maybe you need to hear
*it's okay;*
you're trying your best,
and that is *always* enough.

Maybe you just need to be held today.

*– Hypocritical advice*

I don't know if my arms
are strong enough
to hold you up,
but that doesn't mean
I'm not going to try.

I want to be a pair of gentle hands
that picks up all the pieces cast aside
because I know how that feels –
to be slowly unraveling and falling apart.

Because I've been looking for pieces of myself
I tore away ever since I was eight.

## A Request for More Student Loans

*Sure, we can get you more,* he says,
white teeth plastered in a plastic smile,
the empty eyes of a salesman.

*What are we up to now?* he asks,
and I've already forgotten the number.
I'm swallowed up by the sterile room,
stark LED lights above boring into me,
like a patient laid out in a hospital bed.
I mumble my uncertainty,
but he doesn't hear, and it doesn't matter.

He is the ferryman
and I am one of his passengers.

As he runs the numbers, I look around,
the picture propped on his desk –
his family on vacation in Hawaii,
the golden nameplate,
quotes and inspiration on the walls,
the framed certifications over our heads.

I can't say how long I've been here,
my begging hands outstretched.

The queue to get in snakes right out the door
and off down the hall, and I see them all,
gripping armrests with white knuckles,
sweat streaking down, awaiting his gavel,
anxious to learn if they will eat
ramen for another week
or if next week will be different from the last.

### Orientation

Anxiously, we wait,
tucked tight into a crowded space,
nervous smiles strewn across each face.

Familiar figures
find their place next to one another,
and those of us alone feel it all the more.

What we don't realize
is that here, we're nearly all the same:
uncertain, unproven, and under some
unspoken spell.

We all came here, to the land of the stars,
hoping we might become one ourselves.
Some of us, like me, from far away,

And yet unsaid,
the air is heavy and filled with dread.

We all know we can never truly be friends,
only rivals and competitors and rats,
vying for our positions,
for our place in this unending race,
to achieve our own desires,
all the way to the end.

## What Do You Want?

I stare at the blank pages and wonder
what I really came here for

I want to write screenplays,
filled with memorable characters
who feel relatable and real

I want to live in some little house
overlooking the water,
so on nights I can't sleep, I can step outside
and breathe in the salty air
to remember that this world is very much *alive*

I want to forget about money –
or have *just enough*
to not have to worry about it ever again

I want to be free,
from the overreliance on others,
their expectations and disappointments

I just want them all to be happy with me.

My clammy little six-year-old fingers
gripping an orange ticket stub,
savory buttered popcorn,
cold, crisp soda,
and neon lights along the ground
as we slip in to find our seats.

The shroud of darkness envelopes us,
the only light provided
by the glow of the giant screen,
the booming sound
rumbling in my chest.

Everything outside of this room
*disappears*
and I go with it.

I am wherever they take me.
I feel whatever they make me.

I want to be part of this magic.
The magic that made me believe
*anything* was possible.

I don't know when I gained this strength,
this ability to push past the fear
and take myself up to new heights –
when I became this brave new *me*.

But I'm no longer scared
of all the things I used to be.

Now, somehow, my fears are different;
they have evolved – like me.

## Transparent

Staring at the stars
I look up to, I admire,
from beneath my own veil of scars,
I softly wonder and stew in doubt.

Will I ever get in?
Will I ever belong up there, with them?

Do they see through me?
Everyone here –

Do they know I don't belong?

Do they know the real me?
I'm just a kid
in a little over my head.

Do they see it too?

Am I so obvious?

How much longer will I last
before they see right through?

## Amateur

I have these big ideas inside of me,
pushing up against my ribs.

I want to write the characters
wandering through my head
but I can't seem to give them lines
worthy of being read.

I think if these characters could talk,
they would urge me to give them away
to someone they can trust
to express whatever they have to say.

A better, more seasoned writer
would know how each scene should flow,
would know how to tell their story,
and take ideas wherever they need to go.

I think
all I'm good for
is coming up with ideas
for *better* writers.

### Ghost

Who I was
seems to have followed me here –
gum tracked on my heel
from a thousand miles
and a dozen years away.

I thought a new start
meant that I could leave my past behind.

But I find it in dreams,
some days I hear the words *mom* or *dad*
from other students,
and I find it tearing me apart
at the seams.

I struggle to move past that life before –
It's haunting me, and I think holding me back
from becoming something more.

When will I let it go?

When will I be free of whoever I used to be?

# Uncharted Waters

# PART ONE

There is a maple outside my window;
I look at it every day and I think I know what
it is like to be that tree.

Its leaves gradate in fall,
they shed in winter,
slowly regrow anew in spring,
and love life in summer.

But the tree stays the same,
the trunk, its branches, the roots – they never
move, they never change.

The world makes its inevitable impact on it,
but the tree just goes through the motions,
unable to break the cycle.

### Engagement

Something is wrong with me,
I just know it.

Maybe it's simply who I am,
but I think people notice and wonder
why I'm different.

I am happy with him,
and I am looking forward to spending my life
with him.

But my heart doesn't skip a beat, a trill.
I want to hide – this event isn't for me.
How much more can I pick at my thumb
until it bleeds?

When I think about what led to this point,
all I can say is, this is the natural progression.

I think people want me
to act differently about it –
thrilled, girly, head over heels.

Maybe something is defective in me.

It's something I do,
it's nearly instinct now –
I have no control over it, it's so natural.

I turn off parts of myself
so you'll like me.
I so badly need you to accept me
and I don't think you will if you see all of me.

But maybe if I hide
my dark humor,
my interests,
my opinions you don't share,

I have a shot at being accepted by you.

There is something romantic
about finding a quiet spot in an old building
with musky, outdated furniture
while hundreds of people bustle about outside
around me.

As if I've found my own little nest among
the hive and no one can disrupt me from
my work or my thoughts.

I think about walking a lot;
each step being so small
but you accumulate so many.

I think about how many steps
I must have taken in my life.
Over coarse sand, hot driveways,
soft grass, busy sidewalks,
quiet forests, muffled carpets,

And I wonder how each step
brought me closer to who
and where
I am now.

I wonder how each future step
will bring me close to who
and where
I will be.

We adopted a dog and she's beautiful.
I knew she was perfect the moment I saw her.

The soul in her eyes, quiet and withdrawn,
the trauma of her past,
made me want to show her
full and complete love.

She hasn't always made it easy;
her separation anxiety
resulted in a torn-up textbook
and a door being chewed through.

But when she has an anxiety attack,
we have a ritual.
I curl up with her,
and we watch *The Dick Van Dyke Show*,
and I sing to her,
*da dada da dada*
*dadada dadada*
*dada dada dada dada da wump bum.*

My legs bounce up and down in my seat.

I release the breath I didn't know
I was holding in
and automatically hold it again.

Just a little longer
until I can make a break for it.

Just a little longer
until I can find my place to cry.

Just a little longer
until I can release
and try to feel okay.

Just a little longer.

I'm addicted to comfort.

I recreate the good feelings too much
to the point where the comfort is lost.

I search for new ways to get it
then beat it like a dead horse again.

These new ways
aren't often healthy,
they cost money,
and they usually make me feel guilty after.

*Why can't a little go a long way for me?*

When life is too unbearable to participate
but you're too scared to leave it,
the best thing to do is to become someone else.

I've been the chosen one,
I've seen worlds beyond your comprehension,
I've fought battles no one thought I would win.

I've shared bonds with friends that run
deeper than anything,
I've found love in every way,
and I've proven my capabilities time and again.

Until I put the book down and I remember
I'm just plain ole me.

How many times have I looked at
bushes, trees, and weeds,
and only now have I noticed
the new growth in spring.

The tiny buds that promise new life
and give me a small reason to smile.

A reminder to smell the air after a fresh rain
and look to the sky.

*I am small
in this universe,*

I tell myself.

What a wonderful weight off my shoulders.

202.0 lbs. *I hate myself.*

198.4 lbs. *I hate myself.*
196.9 lbs. *I hate myself.*
194.7 lbs. *I hate myself.*
192.9 lbs. *I hate myself.*
188.8 lbs.

190.3 lbs.
191.5 lbs.
195.0 lbs. *I hate myself.*

187.2 lbs.
182.1 lbs.
179.9 lbs.

182.0 lbs. *I hate myself.*

*144.0 lbs. That's when I'll love myself.*

It's taken over two decades for me to realize
I don't know who I am
truly,
the essence of myself
is nowhere to be found
and for some, that might be exciting –
a chance to build who they want to become.

But it scares me,
my body floating through space
with no soul to inhabit it.

I'm always so unsure,
    too scared to take any steps.
I'm stagnating, paralyzed –
    becoming complacent
    in living this life I don't even want,
watching it pass by as I act out this part
    I realized I never wanted.

I want that to scare me
more than the fear of failing –
    to make me move,
    to wake me, to make me act.

But it doesn't,
and another day passes me by.

I'm trying to hold on to him
by being perfect in any way I can,
at least in front of him.

Whatever acts of service I can provide,
whoever I need to be,
whatever I need to say,
to hold on to the only person who is
still in my life.

*Please just tell me I'm enough.*

## Am I Brave Enough? (Part II)

For as long as I can remember,
I never believed in myself.

If things got hard, I stopped.
If I knew a challenge would appear,
I wouldn't even start.

I picked careers that I idealized:
working on a cruise ship,
being a travel guide,
working in the Library of Congress archives.

But always, I found a way to talk myself
out of them.

I've managed to stumble through life
never really committing much to anything.
And now I'm at a crossroads with my degree.

Do I go further in my education? Do I get my
teaching certificate? I'm perfectly set up for it,
I've taken the prerequisites,
I know the professors,
I know what kind of teacher I would want to be,

but am I brave enough?

Am I brave enough to commit to
the good and the bad,
to a career instead of a job,
to a lifestyle different than what I know?

I tell myself I could graduate, come back, and
get my certificate later
if I want more time to decide.

But I know it's now or never –
I won't come back for this
if I don't do it now.

Am I brave enough?
Am I brave enough?
Am I brave enough?

*Yes*, I tell my imaginary students, *you are!*

But to my own reflection, I say nothing.

I'm doing great,
I've got everything a person could want!

*A dog,*
*a partner,*
*a degree,*
*a part-time, minimum-wage retail job,*
*weight gain,*
*isolation,*
*anxiety medication,*
*alcohol,*
*depression,*
*disassociation.*

I promise, Mom and Dad, I'm so very content
with my life.
If this isn't happiness,
I don't know what is.

Have I told you I live in the middle of nowhere
in a trailer with three-inch-thick walls
that do nothing to keep winter out?

Have I told you we have a woodburning stove
we need to use
unless we want another $300 electric bill?

Did I mention I thought I could chop wood,
but on my first try,
I split an inch in the top of my foot?
Bloody footprints streaked my house
as I fumbled to call for help.
I was alone at the time.
I sat in the bathtub and propped my foot up,
putting pressure on it waiting for the EMTs.

Because if I didn't chop wood,
no one would,
and if I didn't worry about the bills,
no one would,
and there is some type of irony
in a $1,300 medical bill
for foot stitches because of all that.

This feels like it signifies something,
but I'm not sure what.

All I know is I cried the next time I held an axe.

I'm sorry for canceling last minute –
you see, I wanted to go, *really*.
I want to have friends,
haven't I always?

But my house is so safe,
and socializing is so unpredictable.
I just couldn't bring myself to go.

– *Things left unsaid*

If I have a moment of lucidity
and I pull myself out of the haze of
avoidance, expectations, and numbness,

I need to question if –
no,
I *know*
I'm not happy.

But I don't know what is wrong with me
or how to get better.

So, I'll keep telling myself I'm fine,
and I'll fade back into the haze
a little more dissatisfied than before.

You have seen me more at my best
than at my worst.

I admit,
I am afraid,
I am nervous and anxious,
I am weak, and I want to do things
that I know are not good for me,
I am petty sometimes, and jealous too,
I can be my least favorite person.

But I am trying, oh my goodness, I'm trying,
every day,
to be better than the day I was before.
So please, be patient with me,
I am still growing.

It is the natural cycle of the world
that things must get worse
before they get better.

But when you think you're in the worst
and later realize you were wrong,

It is like stepping your foot down
thinking there will be one more step,
and instead
it is a flight of stairs you tumble down.

PART TWO

### Twenty-One

They drink beer and wine,
students splayed out on couches,
pop music pumping along to pass the time.

None of them are even here –
able to let go, drift off and away.
Only I lie awake,
thoughts stuck on the hands of the clock.

I don't have *time* to do this –
to do what they do.

I took a huge gamble, moving down here –
no money, no relatives, no backup plan,
and if this does not work, what will be left?

If I want to make it big, I must double down,
I must be serious – I can't afford
to relax, to let go, to drink.
This is it, now or never.

No time for fun,
not when there's so much work to be done.

When it all comes together,
When that line forms just the perfect rhyme,
When the smile spreads across the reader's face,
When the characters simply write themselves,
When the piece feels like it flows
the perfect pace
with not an ounce of fat,
When the producer or publisher calls
and says they want your work,
they want whatever you have,
and they want it *all*.

*That* is why I write.

*Hello, big sister,*

*I'm calling to check in.*
*How are you doing back home?*
*How are the kids at school? How is the mister?*

*Your little brother is doing just fine,*
*keeping my grades up and staying in line.*
*I go to bed earlier now, just like you asked,*
*and I'm taking better care of myself, so relax.*

*You can rest easy,*
*knowing I'm making good choices.*
*I still don't drink,*
*I still don't party,*
*I still haven't done any drugs,*
*I still write, and I still hope this is all worth it.*

*I know we haven't talked in a couple of days,*
*but I promise I'm still doing okay.*

*I'm sorry to ask — it always feels so rude,*
*but can you please send me some more money*
*so I can buy some food?*

I hear their words, their whispers at my back.
I see their eyes locked onto me,
like vipers, coiled back and poised to attack.

Some kid from a small town.

He's so out of place,
you can see the innocence,
the cluelessness written all over his face.

He won't have a drink – he's such a prude,
he'll never make it here, not with that attitude.

He's still a virgin I hear –
what is he saving it for?

He thinks he's something special,
he thinks he can make it in our world.
How naive.

Go back to your small town, boy.
This place will break you,
you'll see.

*It's only a matter of time.*

There will always be things
you do not know,

So be humble and kind
wherever you go.

## Unworthy

Maybe you think yourself unworthy of love,
but you're wrong.

Through the pitching darkness,
over the twisting bramble,
the broken stones and the hollowed-out bones,
braving the heat of the whitest fires,
*I would come for you.*

My hands were made for healing,
the unseeable wounds, the unspeakable hurts.
So come and take them,
these rugged and calloused palms,
let them hold you tight.
They were born of the earth, too, like you,
they will hold you up into the light.

*You are worth the fight.*

I don't know why,
but I've always seen the best in people,
even when they don't deserve it.

I want to believe that
everyone can be better than they are,
that most of the time – they want to be,
that everyone has the potential.

I know
in some other world
I could have easily become homeless
or addicted to drugs
or committed suicide.

That could have been me
if nobody ever gave me a chance.

So let go your judgment,
loosen your hardened stance.

Not everyone gets a fair shot right out the gate.

*What is your plan B?*
my sister had asked
when I told her
I wanted to move to L.A.
to follow my dreams,
to make it big,
to get paid to write stories
for the rest of my years.

*I have no plan B,*
I declared, in anger and pride,
*This is it. This is all. I will make it.*
*I'm tired of living my life for other people,*
*I'm tired of trying to hide.*

If only I heard the wisdom in her words,
the worry in her heart.
I see it now – but it's all too late.

## Every Day for a Year

In the best suit a college student can buy,
I set my smile and fix my tie.

Twenty crisp résumés,
printed on thick paper,
heavy with importance, packed with promise.
I grip them a little too tight
as I take the bus nearly an hour away,
preparing for yet another fight,

Upbeat songs drum up in my chest,
inflating my fragile confidence.
I clutch it tight
like a child holding a balloon.

Inside the mall, I steel myself
and pick up where I left off yesterday.

I go to every business,
ask to speak to every manager,
repeating the mantra that no job is beneath me.

I'm a team player and a leader, I'm a go-getter,
I'm a self-starter but I can follow direction,
I am whatever they are looking for.

But it doesn't matter what I may be,
because nobody is looking for someone like me.
I enter a store and recognize the faces.
I realize, somehow, in the past three months
I've come full circle, I've been here before.

The final pinprick,
the air hisses out from my balloon.
I try to hold it all in, but it's slipping away –
the confidence, the hope I've built up all day.

I get out and find a new store, a shoe store.
I wonder there, how many times
have I had these same conversations before,
and been shown the door?

My clammy hands
clasp my last résumé,
and I ask to see the manager.

He greets me with a manic smile,
and I return what hollow one I have left.
But he sees right through,
and his words reflect the insecurities
I thought I'd hidden away.

> *That's the best you've got?*
> *You look miserable and tired.*
> *How do you expect to be taken seriously*
>     *if you can't even smile?*
> *Why would I hire someone like you?*
> *You don't look excited to get a job.*

Crumpled and beaten down,
I feel like a child again.
He hands me back the résumé.
>    *Keep this*, he says, *I don't need it.*

## Mirror (Part II)

My face is a stark photograph
tacked up on display.

A ravaged canvas,
lines drawn by an unskilled artist
with shaky hands.

A wood-carved sculpture
with too many bits hacked off,
all harsh corners and sunken pits,
pale and gaunt,
eyes sunk back behind heavy violet lids.

Days and months and years of nights
spent studying more than sleeping,
spent staring at the computer glare
and the walls of words in a textbook.

– *Face of the student body*

### Empty

I've been told, *It's nothing personal,*
but it's hard not to think
I did something wrong
when I've been applying for
months and no one will take me.

Every *I'm sorry to inform you,*
sounds a lot like *You're not good enough.*

The mall is a walk of shame,
passing by places that didn't want me –
a graveyard of résumés.

*I'm sorry, world, but I tried,*
*and I have nothing left for you.*

*I've given you all I have,*
*and I've landed nowhere.*

I'm still falling.
I don't know what else to do.

**Overgrown**

When I was little, I had a problem.

I had a dream I tucked inside.
I fed it love and time and care,
but I hadn't realized I had been pouring in
all my expectations too.

You see, the problem was that it grew
so big it began to tear a hole right through
and now my dream is towering above –
outgrowing the naive dream I used to love.

This roof is much too low,
and who I wanted to be
is just too big now to fit, you know?
Where does the wasted potential fit,
where does it all go?

There's no space left for it here.
How do I let go of everything that I held dear?

I don't know how to stretch my limbs
the way they were meant to be.
And now I question, what did these *dreams*
ever mean to me?

SK WILLIAMS

I have stared too long
in bathroom mirrors
and not known who I am.

I have found myself
in waters
I did not expect to swim.

I do not recognize
this body I'm growing into –
this person I am becoming.

## To Be a Child Again

I lie awake another night in bed,
curled up in a ball, blanketed in memories,
my fingers interlaced behind my head.

I try to take myself back to tranquil reveries.

The bounding spring up off the trampoline,
the summer air rushing by on the swings,
the smell of fresh-baked oatmeal-chocolate-chip,
the inflatable pool waiting for me to take a dip,
feeling unashamedly young and wild and free,
yet picked up by father when I scraped my knee,
yearning desperately for summer all year long,
falling asleep to another old-timey song
on the long drives spent in the back seat,
driving past field after field after field of wheat.

My tears lessen as I slow my weep,
my thoughts soften, and I drift off to sleep.

*Not every day will be like this.*

It's an easy reminder on the hard days,
when you need something to look forward to,

But it's a nice thing to remember
on the good days too.

Cherish the good days
whenever you have them.

### Graduation

I've made it at last,
I'm finally here.

All the work I've done,
all the sacrifices I made,
the anticipation and determination,
over the last three years –

It all amounts to this.

These dreams I've had since I was six
can no longer be dismissed.

*I made it.*

These friends,
once rivals, once competitors,
once thought to be the enemy,
have made it with me all the way to the end

A mutual respect has been earned,
somewhere along the way,
a nod, a shake, a wave,
numbers and ideas exchanged

Maybe I was wrong –
maybe it was always more
than a fearsome competition,
a race to be the first to make it to the red carpet,
to find success
on the other side of the door

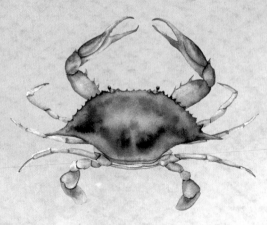

I see the pressure now,
awaiting me ahead,

I see what can happen to me
if I don't end up somewhere,
if I mess around and take it easy
and relax instead.

But I see others, too, all around,
all those peers more fortunate than me,
people who got a head start,
who have all the help that they need,
who have a job even *before* a degree,
or who have parents who know someone.

I know it's wrong,
but it's hard not to feel this envy.

## Why I Keep My Mouth Shut

Have you ever said something
and immediately wished that you hadn't?
It almost felt like it wasn't you who said it.

Maybe you only meant it in jest,
but now that the words spilled from your lips,
you feel them boiling up inside your chest.

You feel them rattling around inside,
scarring at the corners of your brain,
and you can only imagine how heavy they feel,
sinking in through the ears of the person
you did not mean to bring so much pain.

You want to say *sorry*, but what if *sorry*
is not enough to make it okay?
What if they carry these words forever,
weighing them down, until their last day?

I don't know what to do with the words
I wish I never said.
They're still with me, I remember every one.
I turn them over and over and think about
words I should've used instead
and I leave them there,
burning a hole in the back of my head.

## A Million Me's

It seems that everyone wants
something different from me.
And I want to please them all,
but I realize that it's simply an impossibility.

They play tug-of-war with my arms,
and I feel my spine splitting down the middle.

I wish I could split into a million *me*'s –
each *me* could take a different road
and see it through all the way to the end,
and maybe some of them
would meet along the way,
maybe they would be friends.

I think each little *me*
could make so many different people happy.
But instead,
the only *me* is torn and divided,

and a disappointment
is *all* that I can manage to be.

## Breakdown

For the third time this month,
my car broke down,
and it took all I had left in me
to not break down with it.

I can only hold it together for so long.
I don't know what it is about my car,
but something always seems to go wrong.

I don't have the money to fix it all,
I don't know any mechanics or therapists,
I don't know who to call.

I'm crying on the side of the road,
waiting for my car to get towed,
and I can't stop thinking,
I'm heading down the same way
because lately I've been neglecting myself,
and I'm no longer feeling okay.

It takes a toll,
all this work and no time to breathe.

# Beneath The Storm

# PART ONE

## Looking Back

I was small,
and beneath the vast universe,
I knew I was smaller still.
But that all felt okay on the days
when the neighborhood was still and silent –

Fresh-cut grass whispered through the breeze,
and the wind washed my face
as I swung
back
       and
forth
on the swing set in my backyard.

I was small then,
and on some level, I knew
I was a part of the world all around me.

I know now
I'm still small in the universe,
but I miss those days
when it felt *thrilling*
and I long to go back.

## When Did Commitment Become Tolerance?

It's a cold day, and our thin walls
don't protect us enough from the chill.
We spend most of our day in separate rooms
while I try to stay warm with too many layers.

I can't seem to stop shivering
but our heating bill was too much last month.
He won't chop the wood for the fireplace
and when I tried, I sliced my foot.

So, I sit on the couch, alone and cold
in a house I never wanted to move to
in a town far from everything
and I sip my noon o'clock wine
and wonder what I should make for dinner.

I have a bunch of friends.
They always welcome me
and never tire of my visits.

They make me feel included,
and I laugh with them easily.

I watch them over and over again,
I can't seem to say goodbye –
but could you blame me?

Captain Picard takes me on wild adventures,
the Petries soothe me with idealization,
Chuck reminds me I'm always capable of more,
and Planet Express lulls me to sleep each night
so I don't get lost in my thoughts.

Does it matter if all my friends are fictional?
*I don't really seem to have a choice.*

### Imposter

On the first day of seventh grade,
I was so scared to start a new school
that my mom told me, *Fake it 'til you make it*,
and that worked out for me back then.

But it's harder to do it now,
and I'm more frightened than ever;
I can't fake paying rent,
I can't fake having a job,
I can't fake being happy – not forever.

*Will I ever make it?*

It's constricting, digging into me.
It's a painful reminder every second of
what I am no longer.

I don't want to admit it to myself
but there's no denying it –
the whole world can see
I'm not as thin as I used to be.

My parents always said my metabolism would
catch up to me.
I guess it caught me and I'm stuck in
the vice grip of my too-tight jeans,
longing for the hugging embrace
of my leggings.

I guess I'm growing up
and growing out of what I used to be.

It's what happens
when you get an English degree –
you go from job to job,
working in a bank,
at a bookstore,
for an optometrist,
in a plastic manufacturing company,
and for a real estate team.

Not the dusty glamor of old archives
or ancient libraries doing research.
Not traveling the world as
an explorer's bookish assistant,
or unraveling some great mystery.

Things never work out the way
we idealize.

But every step gets us closer
to where we need to be
even if it doesn't always make sense.

*Remember how you said sometimes*
*people need to make sacrifices for relationships?*
he asked.

*Yes.*

*Well, that's what I'm asking you to do.*
*It doesn't matter if you need to get drunk first.*
*But if we don't start doing it soon,*
*things are only going to get worse from here.*
*Do you understand?*

What can I even say in response?

My body is stone,
curled up,
faced away,
hardly breathing.

He gets into bed
and runs a hand over my thigh
under the covers.

*I'm asleep, I'm asleep, I'm asleep.*

My jaw aches from clenching.

*I'm asleep, I'm asleep, I'm asleep.*

But even if I was, nightmares haunt my dreams.
Dark shadows circling the room,
waiting for me to give away any sign
I see them.
I can, without opening my eyes,
but can't let them know.
They'll hurt me if they find out.

New friends
bring new perspectives
and make you realize
maybe things that are normal

*shouldn't be.*

A tentative thrill pulses through my fingers
as I walk up to the bar
in the dark, cold night air.
I'm meeting coworkers for drinks,
people I really like.

I think I could call them friends;
*I hope they would call me that.*

They wave me over,
big smiles in the soft lamplight,
and my heart swells –
this is what it feels like to be
around people who want to be around me.

The night flies by with stories and laughs,
drinks and food, memories, and promises,
and I can't believe how lucky I am –
to be surrounded by people
who I have fun with.

*I forgot what it felt like.*

I'm buried down beneath a whisper.

I don't know where it all went wrong.

It's as if I remember getting in the car,
but I don't remember the drive.
Days blurred into months,
and months into years, and now
I don't like who I've become or who I'm with
or what I'm doing –

*What am I doing?*

This isn't right,
this isn't me,
but do I even know who I am anymore?

I think it's time I step back –
*reevaluate*
*reinvent.*

I need to *refocus.*

## Am I Brave Enough? (Part III)

I am done. I want a divorce.
It's been so long since I've loved him,
and I don't know who he is anymore.

But we're so intertwined –
marriage, house, dog and cat, one car.
It's what I know, and I can't afford to live alone.

But am I brave enough to try?
Am I brave enough to hurt him,
to live on my own for the first time,
to break our entire lives?

Am I brave enough to face the judgment?
To admit I haven't been happy
since before the wedding,
but didn't even realize.
To admit all the wrong I contributed.
To admit how weak I've been.

I'll never know. Because I wasn't brave enough.
Because he beat me to it and asked for one first.
He told me how I'd hurt him.
How I'd wronged him.
How I'd manipulated and embarrassed him.

Am I brave enough
to tell him what he did to me?
The fear that lives inside,
that he could never see?
The self-doubt, the blame, that he instilled –
*no.*

I couldn't add to the pain he needed to express.

Looking back,
I wish I was brave enough to stand up for me.

No responsibilities,
no work, no cares –
let's get boozy tonight.

Let the whiskey get our brains fuzzy,
let our skin tingle,
let the conversation flow uninhibited,
let our laughs be loud and unashamed.

Let's stumble to get the next round –
who cares if it's a good idea.
We're having fun
and living in the moment matters, right?

We won't always be able to do this,
and we haven't been able to for so long.

Let's just share some drinks and some songs
and get lost in the fun.

It all came out,
all that I hid from
my family and friends

All my unhappiness, sadness, and rage.

I expected to be told,
*It was all my fault*
*I should have tried harder*
*I should have been better*

Because that's what he always told me,
and that's what the counselor said too.

It all came out,
all that I hid from
my family and friends

All their unhappiness, sadness, and rage.

At my situation
and not being there for me more
and wanting to be there now
*to tell me they love me,*
*support me,*
*validate me.*

It was the light
I didn't know how badly I needed.

How many times
have I watched fresh green buds emerge from
barren trees
on walks to and from so many places?

How many times
have I baked in the sun like a lizard
and relished the warmth hugging my skin?

How many times have I inhaled a crisp autumn
breeze and felt the tingle of fear from
an overactive imagination around Halloween?

How many times have I admired the snowfall
with a hot cup of comfort
and a book I couldn't put down if I tried?

Time passes, seasons ebb and flow
and as I grow,
I cherish the things that will never change.

I feel it
from somewhere in the depths,
a reserve I thought I tapped out –

A readiness,
a new resolve,
a second wind.

This is a new phase
and I'm ready for it.
I know I have the strength;
I know it'll be hard.

But despite my fear
I know it'll be worth it.

When two plants grow in the same pot,
their roots get intertwined;
they live together happily
basking in the sun and soaking up the water.

But when these plants grow big enough,
the pot gets cramped and tight.
They fight for space to grow
and will strangle the other
in order to survive.

The other becomes a weed
and the happiness is gone.

Anyone can become cruel
if they grow together in
space that is too small.

There is a joy in being alone,
in having complete control of
what you do,
what you eat,
what you say

There is a comfort in being alone,
in having
the bed be a safe space,
the room to breathe,
the silence to think

There is a healing that comes in being alone,
when you answer only to yourself,
where you can try self-love,
where you can sit in peace

*There is freedom*

# PART TWO

## Twenty-Three

What does it mean, to be eighteen,
to be twenty-one, to be twenty-three?
Am I different now or is it just
another year, another me?

I realize I've become the starving artist
I always strived to be,
an old coat at the back of the closet,
tired and tattered, waiting to be worn.

This pale body has grown thin on time,
tired of excuses, anxiously searching
for some reason why I have not made it,
angry with myself for not doing better.

I don't know
how to get from *here* to *there*.
Where do I go after this?
Why wasn't I prepared?

How do I come to terms with the truth?
This is not how I thought it would be.
When do I turn my back on these dreams?
When do I trade childhood fantasies
for a happier, healthier, wealthier me?

### Blank Paper

I struggled a lot today,
found I had nothing important to say,
and so I didn't write anything at all.

Page after page, I turned,
hoping the next would pull words out of me,
but nothing whispered to me in the day,
and nothing came to me in the night.

The blank paper is filled
with judgment,
the only metaphor presented back to me
is a cruel and perfectly fitting one that says,

*You haven't done enough*
*to earn the success*
*you think you deserve.*

Maybe I'm a coward
because I used to have a dream
that I could make the whole world bright
and now I just want to feel all right.

Everything is just too heavy,
my shoulders are screaming,
my head is cold and sweaty,
and I just want to lay it all down.

I've grown so tired of carrying
the weight all on my own,
of nobody else believing in me.
I can't do this anymore – not alone.

I'm a fool and I'm tired and trapped.
I feel so lonely in this sickly dream.
Everyone knew I wouldn't make it –
everyone but me.

## The Big 5-0

It's a big day for me,
a day that only comes once in my life:
my first student loan bill arrived.

It's due in a month,
the same day as rent.
I've got time, they say,
but it feels like it's already spent.

Fifty thousand is a lot of dollars.
I don't know what I was thinking,
but I don't know how I'll ever
make *that* much money in *this* life.

In high school, it took me a year
to save up a thousand.
Maybe if I'm lucky, by the time I turn fifty,
I'll be debt free.

I have to make it big;
I have to hit all the stars I shoot for;
I have to sell a million books;
I'm in too deep to go back.

I hear the choir of *I told you so*'s
but I already know, oh, I already know —

I made a mistake
betting on myself.

## The Quiet One at the Party

I knew the moment I pulled up,
there were at least thirty people
already packed inside.

I can hear the weight of them
pressing up to the walls,
through the steel of my car doors,
the bass rumbling deep in my chest.

Facing myself in the mirror,
I consider one last chance to turn around –
to head back to my apartment
and say I never even came,
but the eyes staring back at me
tell me I'm a coward if I don't go in.

I step out and every step forward
is more cumbersome than the one before.
The windows rattle with excitable energy
waiting for release,
the low booming within
setting an anxious expectation of what lies
beyond the threshold ahead.

I open the front door,
and feel the release of all the pent-up energy
inside, blasting me back on my heels,
making me second-guess entering in.
But someone sees me and waves me over.

Voices are fragile beneath the ocean of sound,
faces are a few dozen blurs
moving back and forth across the room,
and I struggle to keep up with the movement,
swimming just beneath the murmurs abound.

The smiling host reaches out and
grabs the bottle in my clammy hands.
I don't even remember bringing it in.
He claps me on the back and motions me on
and my body obeys
because it doesn't know what else to do,

And in ten minutes, I am at the windows,
petting some dog, giving it my attention,
anxious bricks strapped to both of my feet,
my words have left me
and my wide eyes are looking out to the street,

The voices and faces behind me a hollow din,
I stare at some plant, hoping they don't notice
that I don't belong here –
that I am not like them.

Keep it together.

They can't see you falling apart inside.

### Mirror (Part III)

Awake, alert,
I rise before the sun,

I strap on my shoes,
ready to take on the day,
and I run and run –
pushing myself farther and faster,
until my mind slips away.

Breath finds rhythm,
feet move in time to song,
and with the whole world drowned out,
I find I could do this all day long.

Here, alone in my head,
I am in control.

I stare at myself in the mirror,
after the five miles have been overcome,
sweat glistening, ragged breath, red-faced,
shaky smile on my lips,
and I realize – I feel a little better,
but there's still more work to be done.

*What would happen if I didn't pay my loans?*

I don't have a car, I don't have a home.
What would they take from me, I wonder?

Would they pry away a limb or take my body,
would they throw me in jail on a whim?
A twenty-three-year-old kid
who couldn't afford bail, much less a hobby.

I wonder if they are proud of themselves
for the system that they have made,
the sprouting, thriving debt I can't cut down –
the person I used to be has begun to fade.

I've been trying to scramble out of this hole
I didn't realize I was climbing into,
crumbling beneath the weight of this debt
and feeling my lungs filling up with dirt,
with so many regrets.

*I'm so deep in the depression that*
*I can't see the earth up above.*

Every now and then
I feel the need
to do something reckless and stupid
just to remind myself
I'm in control of my life
and I can choose where to take it.

**Stranded**

I broke free from my shell, here on this shore.

I watched everyone grow up and grow out,
carried off by waves, to go somewhere far away
and become something more.

Every day feels like another year
and I wonder now – why didn't *I* go?

I've been stuck in the same apartment
for the last three years, with nothing to show
for all the blood, sweat, and tears.

They all moved on and got married,
had children, settled into stable careers,
while I tread water,
weighed down by my fears.

*Is this how friendships really end?*

*Not in some big fight,*
*but silently, softly fading away into the night?*

Is this a part of growing up,
of growing old,

this solitude?
This flaking and breaking, this falling away
of all the parts of yourself
you thought were permanent?

Your friends, your family,
your hope for happiness?

Who will I be
when I'm left threadbare?
When all the temporary components
are dug out of me
and only my skeletal roots remain?

Am I to be an old, tired, and lonesome man,
writing stories beside the sea
with nobody to read them, besides me?

## Circadian Blues

Violet skies surround reddened, tired eyes.
I want to sleep, but the brain can't seem to ever
finish counting the sheep.

This has gone on far too long and become
the established rhythm, an endless cycle.
I no longer know how to reset,
how to turn back the dial,
how to let go of all the pressure,
how to forget.

I spend more hours lying in bed,
letting stressful thoughts run rampant
through my head,
than I do with my eyes closed
and my smile easing on,
in the dreamscape, meandering along.

And now the long sleepless nights
have cut into the stark bright days –
the sunlight a disturbing intruder,
on the sagging sleepy eyes
of someone who no longer feels okay.

Everything feels heavy,
my eyes and my head pulled down,
down deep, deep into the ground.

## Tightrope

Family gatherings have become
a precarious walk over embers and eggshells.

It has been so long since they've seen me,
they're bound to bring up sensitive topics.

The little things they remember
from however long ago
only serve as reminders
of my shortcomings.

*How is that script coming along
that you mentioned writing last year?*

*How are you and that girl doing?
Have you popped the question yet?*

*I hear you graduated.
Have you gotten a job?*

If they ask the wrong questions,
what will I tell them?
Will I lie?

I find myself getting dressed every morning
in the same
thick weighted coat of shame,
a constant disappointment
to everyone, but *especially* to me.

My words feel too heavy to hold in my throat.
I used to be able to lie,
to tell them the things they want to hear,
but it's all caught up with me.
These facts are no longer little things
that I can conceal for long.

*I didn't get the job.*
*They went another direction.*
*I need to ask for money again.*
*I need help with rent.*
*I might need to move back in.*

Give me a little time
to free myself
from the me
everyone wants me
to be.

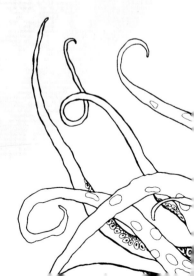

## Treading

Why do we have to figure it all out
when we're only eighteen –
when we don't even know yet who we are?

Everyone told me
to go to college to get a job,
and I tried all that, but I didn't succeed.
The debt washes in every day now, like waves,
and it's up to my knees and it won't go away.

Why didn't this work out for me
when it worked for you?
Why am I not okay?
And why is my skin turning blue?

Slowly, I'm running out of my fight,
the debt is filling my lungs.
Soon, my weight will be pulling me down.
I have only bought myself *time*
in all my flailing around.

I want it to be over, to say I've had enough,
but this is not allowed.
What kind of life is this?

Treading water until I drown.

**The Storm**

Rumbling and quaking,
crashing and breaking,
the ripples of light,
the howl of the wind,
the tempestuous waters
shaking the life out of my fight.

The storm has overtaken me.

I don't know how long
I expected to last,
but this has been coming;
it was only a matter of time
before the waves crashed over me,
before it was too much to hold together.

My strewn-together ropes
have come undone,
my frame is broken,
my sails are ablaze,
and I've given in at last
to whatever the seas
have in mind for the rest of my days.

Whatever it is now,
whatever is ahead,
I am at its mercy.

Sinking, flailing, pulled down, down, down . . .

I don't know how it all got to this point,
but I can't face the pressure.

I feel myself compacting,
falling apart and writhing within,
my ribs poking into my heart,
my shoulder smashing my chin,
my fingers bent back into my belly,
there's no air left to let in.

Down so far in the deep,
I don't know how to escape the fear, the dread,
the water seeping into my mouth,
filling up my lungs,
and rising into my head.

I am powerless beneath the weight of it all,
my feet more anchors than fins,
incapable of slowing my fall.

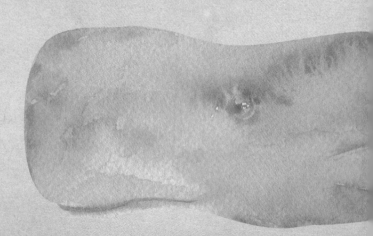

## Whale Song

Whales groan and drift by on either side,
haunting and hypnotic,
and somehow humbling, reminding me
no matter how great the pressure,
there are still so many things
bigger than this – bigger than me.

With their rumbling melody
so low and deep, soothing my soul,
I can feel my body uncurling,
like sails unfurling.
I can see, far down below,
the heavy pressure, the anxiety,
shed from my body,
sinking deep into the depths.

I don't even remember
letting go.

*What could I be, without them*
*weighing me down?*

## Naive

How much do dreams cost?

I always thought
that hope was enough.
A little hope to carry me on,
to push me through, to make it big –
but now I know that's just not true.

It took everything I had
and I lost it all because I was too busy
worrying, asking myself –
how can I just stand tall?
How can I be seen over the rest of them?
How can I be seen with the best of them?

Just a little hope.
It got me through so much before,
but when I took a chance on myself
it simply wasn't enough.

*The dream cost me the rest of my life.*
*It will never be mine again.*

I feel shame in moving back home,
back to people who never believed in me.

I feel like part of me has died,
the part that believed in hopes and dreams,
the part of me that was resilient,
that said I can be anything – I know I can –
if only I believe in *me*.

There is comfort, too,
I admit – in letting go.

I feel like my legs can finally rest,
now that I have abandoned my quest.

Every little thing I own
fits conveniently into the back
of a little truck.

Maybe that says something about me
or something about my bad luck.

Maybe I'm meant to be the punch line
of some cruel joke,
getting a job at a bookstore
back home,
where your dreams are so tired
they do not visit you anymore

I spend all my days looking at spines,
wishing it were me
who wrote these pages,
fingers tracing over well-written lines

Some part of me still wishes,
still steps from bookcase to bookcase
and imagines one day,
maybe I will join them there,

Maybe this little dream
could find some space.

# At The End

# PART ONE

## Am I Brave Enough? (Part IV)

Am I brave enough to see
how growing and self-love aren't
just for me?
If I were to heal, it could bring joy
to other people.

Am I brave enough to believe
that I own a space in others' hearts?
That I am not so easily
discarded as I thought?

Am I brave enough to walk
through the memories,
pain, and self-loathing

With faith that on the other side
is laughter, confidence, and light?

Am I brave enough to love
the one person I never could
and smile at her in the mirror
with nurturing acceptance?

Looking back,
I was so low, I didn't know
how I managed day-to-day
for so long,

But I did.
*What does that say?*

Am I finally able to see
that bravery was always inside me?

As I look back, I wonder how I got here
How I managed under the depths,
holding my breath,
my lungs about to burst,
screaming as the
air bubbles floated up and away from me

I wonder how I made it to the surface
where the sun warms my face and
the water is no longer threatening –
but soothing

I must not remember much of the journey
but I can only surmise

That I was stronger than I realized.

Without even realizing,
I've climbed so many mountains
that once seemed to tower over me
but now seem like nothing more than
the foothills they truly are.

This journey hasn't always been easy,
I haven't always taken the right path,
and I know
I'll continue to make mistakes as I go.

But my experience has built up within;
I feel more prepared for the road ahead
than I ever have before.

When did I become so capable?
When did I become more self-assured?

I felt so small at the start
and now —
now I am climbing mountains,
voyaging the seas,
flying with the birds.

I'm looking forward to the growth ahead of me
and to the person I will continue to become.

The universe is inside you.
Oh yes, dear,
the vast expanse of the known
and unknown, the galaxies far and wide,
the deep roots of the trees,
the power of the stars,
the currents of the oceans –
are all things that make up
you.

*– Your body is made of ancient wisdom*

## Falling Behind

Oh wow, you bought a house!
Yeah, that's great,
I'm so happy for you!

       No, no, we haven't bought yet,
       you know how expensive it is . . .

Oh nice, you're going on vacation!
How many countries did you say?

       No, our last vacation
       was a weekend trip to the coast . . .

Congratulations, I'm so happy you two
are getting married!
Oh, that's an expensive venue!

       Oh yeah, we're planning a small
       backyard ceremony –
       it's what we can afford . . .

Oh, you got a job!
Wow, that pays really well!

       More than double what I make . . .

No kidding, you're pregnant?
That's amazing!

       We aren't sure
       when or if we want to try . . .

*What am I doing wrong?*

*Why does everyone else seem so much
more successful than me?*

It took me a long time to realize
you don't have to do it all
the way your parents did.

It was a different time
and they were different people.

It's okay if it takes a while to
settle down,
buy a house,
have kids,
start over,
get better.

Everyone does it all differently
and it works out just fine.

You have to find your own way
so just take your time.

I was passionate for passion.
I wanted to feel it hot and burning
in my heart, my stomach, my bones.

I wanted to feel so moved by something
that it would be my calling in this life.

But as I continued to grow, it never ignited.
I wanted to make this passion my livelihood;
I wanted to make a difference
every day of my life.

*Something had to be wrong with me,*
I thought.

My mom,
she said sometimes you need to do things
to afford you your small passions.

I didn't want to admit she was right
but it's true, you know.

I have my dog, I have my family, friends,
crochet, conservations, walks,
books, and writing.
I have my passions.

Hi, younger me,

I'd ask how you are, but I know.
I know you feel lonely, and I know you try not
to feel at all some days. I know you feel more
anxious about everything all the time compared
to everyone around you. I know you feel direc-
tionless and paralyzed by fear to do anything
wrong so you do nothing at all.
I know you feel worthless, and unseen.
I want you to know *I* see you. And I love you.

I see you every day in the mirror, and though
you look back, you can't see me. But I am here,
I always was, and always will be. I will always
be your friend. You will survive the storm.
You will be proud of yourself.
You will be happy.
I can promise you these things.

Love always,
Older you

In middle school, I was the girl who
went to the bookstore and hoped
a cute boy would come up to me
and we'd hit it off and
live happily ever after

But life rarely happens the way
you have it planned in
your head

Instead, I worked in a bookstore
and I trained a cute new hire
on the cash register
and we became best friends

Until one day, we realized we
loved each other a little more
than just platonically and
we lived happily ever after.

There is no shame in making mistakes.
This is the time to make them –
they're how you grow.

Don't allow yourself to get stuck
in a relationship because you
don't want to admit things changed.

That isn't the mistake,
it's the *staying* that is –
if it doesn't make you happy.

And if you feel you need permission to
feel the way you do,
this is it. *Your feelings are valid.*

And if you feel you need a sign
to take the steps you've been dreading,
this is it. *I know you can do it.*

I promise you, you are brave enough.

I thought I was getting better,
I thought I was moving on,
but these phrases still echo in my mind

*You called me a monster*

*You made me learn I could never be with*
*someone who has anxiety and depression*

*You messed me up*

And I wonder, was it truly all my fault?
Will I do it all over again without realizing it?

They say I look happier,
which is funny because I tried so hard
to look happy before when I wasn't.

I should've known
hiding my emotions was never my strong suit.

They say I look happier,
which is funny because I never wanted
to start over from scratch again.

But perhaps there is joy
in a fresh start.

They say I look happier,
which is true, because I'm with you now
and I finally know what it means to be loved.

182.0 lbs.
179.6 lbs.
178.3 lbs.
176.2 lbs. *I love myself.*
175.9 lbs. *I love myself.*
175.1 lbs. *I love myself.*
173.6 lbs. *I love myself.*
172.2 lbs. *I love myself.*

173.7 lbs.
175.2 lbs. *I still love myself.*

I admire people who love themselves,
every last wrinkle, roll, and hair.
So why can't I be like that too?

I want to try; I want to look at myself
in the mirror and think, *hey beautiful*,
and mean it.

So, I have been.
And I feel a little silly sometimes,
but it's been working. And you know what?

I think I'm starting to believe it.

## Anxiety These Days Looks Different

I don't show up somewhere
fifteen minutes early and sit in my car for
ten of those minutes rehearsing how
to look casual and confident.

I don't have panic attacks on the
nightly and wonder why I'm so
tired the next morning.

I don't stress about not being
exact and accurate
about every single little thing.

Instead, I get a little nervous shopping
by myself, but I still do it.

I get a little nervous talking on the phone,
but I still do it.

I get jittery and shaky in anticipation
of something I don't want to do
and still do it . . . half the time.

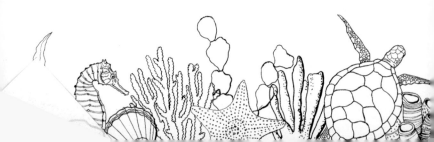

The wetness on your face,
salty and sorrowful,
is anything but a sign of weakness.

It doesn't mean failure
or regression
or incapability.

It is a natural physiological response
of your soul.
It is a release of what you must
not carry anymore.
It is a sign of growth, strength, and humanity.

Be patient with yourself.

Love looks different for everyone
but for us, love looks like:

- Suggesting the same things
  because you're usually on the same page
- Finding ways big and small to
  constantly surprise each other
- Showing an interest and active
  engagement with each other's hobbies
- Agreeing we should stop ordering pizza
  and then ordering it again
- Code words to communicate
  when it's not always easy to
- Being good at the things the other
  isn't as confident in
- Always allowing the tears to flow
  and always catching them with a hug
- Never going to bed angry,
  even if you want to sometimes
- Looking at obstacles as something
  to be overcome as a team
- The evolution of pet names that
  make sense to no one else

It is so easy to see myself as disposable –
an unimportant afterthought.

Inconvenient, or convenient
depending on the situation.

Unimpressive, unremarkable, unlovable.

But in reconnecting with the people
I've pushed away – the people who
I *knew* felt this way, I learned something.

I was *wrong*.
The only one who ever thought those
things about me
was *me*.

Time is funny –
or rather, my perception of it is.
It crawls by agonizingly slow
or races at the speed of light
and I am a passenger to it all.

Four years ago, I never thought I would be
where I am now.
I thought I would never achieve
the things I've achieved.

But look at me:
homeowner, married, author, crocheter,
lucky, grateful, lover, curious, strong.

Time took me here,
and I made these things happen.

*Don't forget to be proud of yourself.*

I know I'm not quite thirty.
I probably still have a lot of time
left on this earth.

I have a lot of wisdom, strength, and confidence
to develop still.
I have experiences on the horizon
that will change me drastically.
I have people in my life
I'll continue to grow with
and people yet to meet.

It excites me to see who I will become.
I know whoever she is, she'll be *magnificent.*

By no means are we at the end of a journey.
Like the whale migrations, we have a
destination, but only until the time comes
to head for the next one.

The sun warms my skin like a gentle hug.
A breeze plays with my hair,
tangling it slightly.
Rain drops feel cold and plump
as they hit my face.
The smell of cottonwood sits thick in my nose.
Snow falling fast, gentle,
and silent is a special joy.
New buds, pink and soft,
emerge in the overcast.
The sidewalk is hard
and familiar under my feet.

And I am here.
Viscerally, fully, awake, alive, and *here*.

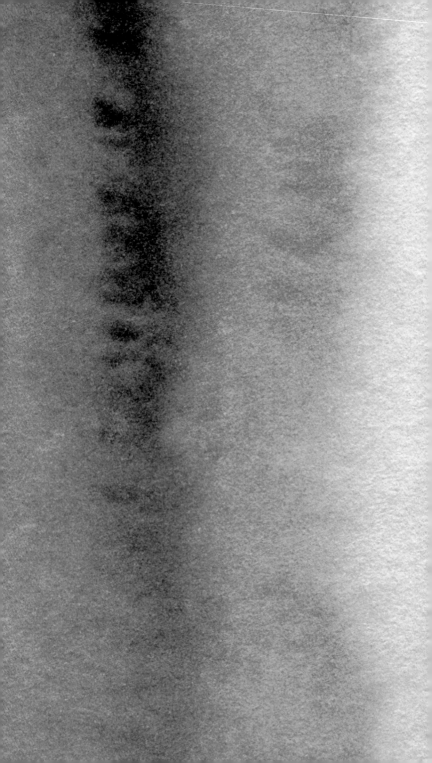

PART TWO

## Twenty-Five

For too long,
I let salt water spill into my lungs,
every day another disappointment
at how long it was taking
to climb the rungs.

I thought if I made my way up
just a little bit higher,
eventually it would all work out,
but then, looking back, looking down,
I was always overflowing with doubt.

I didn't make it
nearly as far as I hoped I would,
not at all,
but I'm still high enough now
that I will get hurt if I fall.

Today I keep hearing
that I'm *only* twenty-five,
still so much time left ahead of me,
still so many reasons to be grateful
for being *alive*.

But I think something drastic
needs to change –
my goals, my dreams, my priorities,
they all need to be rearranged.

I need to just let go,
I need to be okay with
taking things slow.

**Epiphany**

Maybe these written words
don't have to be
the *most* important thing.

Maybe they don't need to feed me,
to put a roof over my head,
to pave my path into the future,
but they can go back
to being a little secret *escape* instead.

Long ago,
these words wrapped around me,
warm and tender,
and taught me I could be vulnerable;
they taught me that
I was safe to surrender.

Maybe I can go back to that place again.

And find them waiting for me,
welcoming me, like an old friend.

Things I want to do before I'm thirty:

- Publish a book (maybe even two)
- Be debt free (or at least close to it, on the right track)
- Live on my own
- Have a financially stable job
- Have at least $10,000 in savings
- Be more in shape – lose weight
- Be on track to clear skin
- Know how to cook at least a dozen good recipes
- Get married – but only if I meet the *right* person

I didn't want to go back to school,
to get another degree, to take out more loans,
to pursue a career that never felt like *me*

But I read my own words
and realize maybe it's something I need to do,
to find my way back,
to relieve the pressure,
to open myself up
to learn something new

The truth is,
you can *always* reinvent yourself,
you can *always* admit when you were wrong
or start over,
even if that means your dreams
must wait a little while longer

When you know you are meant for more,
it is tough to wade through the muck,
your heart – your soul is screaming,
*This isn't good enough,*
and you can't help feeling stuck.

This isn't you,
it isn't right, it isn't easy,
you're wasting your time and potential,
on something that doesn't speak to you –
that doesn't feel essential.

Sometimes we need to be humble,
getting our knees and our fingers dirty
while we stumble,
while we're planting seeds.

Remember why you're here
if this is what you really want to do,
remember why you began this journey,
and remember – all this hard work –

*this is for you.*

Some days,
the words find a way inside,
slipping down the back of my brain
and tugging my mind away
from slowly going insane.

I jot down poems
in the margins of lecture notes,
writing lines
on the backs of tests.

I am anywhere and everywhere
but *here*.

I cannot help myself –
it's the only way
my mind can become clear.

## Joy

I found myself smiling
at the giggles and hushed
conspiratorial murmurs and grins
of a young couple on the bus

I used to flinch at sudden laughter,
instinctively believing
it was always
at my expense

A conditioned trait,
learned as a bullied child,
etched deep into my muscle memory
even after the wounds had healed,
so hard to untangle
from untainted truth

*This* is growth,
a better place than I ever knew,
where I can smile and feel safe
in the delight of others

Allow yourself
those stolen moments,
deep breaths, and little smiles,
those days you let go
even just a little while.

When you put in the work,
it's okay to relax, too,
without feeling guilty.
You don't have to work yourself to death
like they used to work *you*.

There is no shame in resting your body,
giving yourself time to nourish your soul;
this life goes by much too quickly
to spend it all
raking yourself over the coals.

Day in and day out,
people come into the bookstore,
picking up stories,
asking me what this or that one is about —

I am a ranger, a guide, a ferryman,
taking strangers aboard my vessel,
showing them the outlandish dreams of others,
new worlds, new wonders, new experiences,
and profound questions with which to wrestle

I am good at this, I have come to learn,
but *someday*, I think to myself,
looking over all these old oaken shelves,
*I will be more than another guide,*
*but an author too —*
*I'll live among my friends,*
*and be a reader's new experience*
*like one of you*

### Borrowed Confidence

My best friend read my poetry
and said I should share
my words with others
but I don't know –

I never thought my main character
would be *me*.

I don't know if I'm brave enough
to let everyone inside.
What if they see that I'm different?
What if they don't like what they find?

I'll take a chance,
her borrowed confidence
brimming within
but I'll admit – I'm afraid.
I only hope that people
can relate to where I've been.

For some reason,
it's easier for me to believe in myself
when someone else believes in me too

I will never again shame you if you fail.
Never again will I put you down
if all your hard work doesn't prevail.

I am proud of all the things you've done,
all the battles you've fought –
whether you have lost or won.

I am so proud of you, that you stood tall
even when you felt so little, so incapable,
so unworthy, so small.

You are capable of great things, you know.

You always knew –
but somewhere on the way, you forgot.
You forgot to be proud, to be grateful
for the little things you did
while you were shooting for the clouds.

You forgot to let yourself be happy.

Please, just let yourself be happy.
You've earned it.

– *Words I should have told myself sooner*

Every moment of every day,
you can be a different person,
becoming someone new along the way.

As the old parts of you wither and flake,
they fall out of you like baby teeth
and new growth sprouts in their place.

You might find yourself conflicted,
your old ideals incompatible with new ones
you are forming.

Every day, every moment,
you must decide for yourself
who you want to be *now*.

You have to be willing to change,
to recognize you were not always right,
to forgive whoever you were yesterday,
to be better tomorrow,
to let go of the mistakes you made today,
and let them fade with the waning light.

Don't be afraid to let go of certain parts of you.

And be patient with yourself;
you will be okay.

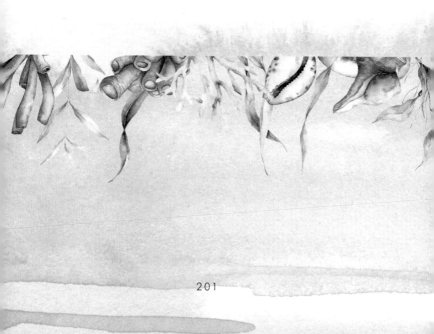

## Tree Rings

We lie together in the dark,
legs strewn out lazily,
wind kissing our cheeks,
and curious eyes
learning the lines of our palms,
the same indentations that have been there
every single day of our lives.

Our heads nestle together
against the base of an old tree,
whose rings were gathered
by each year of its life.

We reflect on the wisdom
drawn from these markings
so different from our own,
each gained from an unforgettable moment
captured in time,
as we unknowingly imprint another line,
another ring around the tree,
one which will hold this new moment
forever.

### Explorer

When you are young,
you are made of more dreams than memories.

You are a world of possibilities,
infinite paths and infinite doors,
all just waiting to be explored.
You can be anyone or anything you want to be.
You can cross the country,
you can follow the winds,
you can take to the sea,
or, if you want,
you can stay wherever you are.
You are malleable and adaptable.
You are choices and chances,
and no matter what you decide,
you can always change your mind.
You can be someone new
with every morning you wake.

Be patient with yourself
and become whoever you want to be.

And when you grow old,
you don't have to leave your youth behind.
There are always new parts of yourself to find.

## Déjà Vu

Here I am again,
the day of my second college graduation,
five years later and, somehow, I did it again,
though this one will be different from the last.

I will not walk this time, but I will *run*.

I am no longer haunted by
some ghost from my past,
and for the first time in my whole life –
I no longer feel like a burden to *anyone*,
no longer wrestling with what I want
and who I am.

I know who I am now,
and I feel the pressure shed,
the expectations wrenched free.

The truth is – whatever I thought,
the pressure always came from *me*.

It feels good to let go – it feels easier to run.
I can be whoever I want
and that will be good enough.

### Deep Breaths

Every day, another penny,
every day, another debt,

Trembling beneath the weight of the storm,
seasick and weary and soaking wet,
my dreams grew tired and worn,

But I've broken free from the thunderclouds
and now everything is so much clearer,

Some of the debt is paid,
and even though there's plenty more
on its way,
I realize now,
everything will be okay

One day at a time,
it's simply
the best that you can do

Someday, I promise,
this debt, this weight,
none of it will have any more power
over you

I found your hands in the dark
when I was stumbling around,
forgetting who I was
with everything going wrong.

You found me down there
and you showed me
that I was just the same as you.

You kissed my lips
and breathed life back into my lungs,
hope back into my heart.

Thank you
for believing in me,
I'm starting to believe too.

I catch myself
comparing my experience
to everyone else.

But they are different.
I am different.

That's something I often need to remember.

Things will work themselves out
in their own time.
The only pressure I'm feeling
is the pressure I'm putting on myself
to get it all together.

But you know what?
I will get there when I get there.
I will get there when I'm ready.

Until then, this is good enough for me.

Things nobody teaches you
that you just have to learn for yourself:

- College doesn't guarantee you a job
- You'll lose some of your best friends
- You'll make new ones – some better
- Some days, ice cream will be the only thing to look forward to
- Some days, ice cream won't be enough
- You're going to fall down a lot
- The little things mean so much more than you realize
- You might have to wait on some tables before you get the job you want
- You're going to disappoint people (*including yourself*)
- You won't be able to make everyone you care about happy
- That's okay
- You will be okay – even when it feels like your whole world is in pieces
- You are always enough

### Las Vegas, 2018

When the call comes in,
I do not hear it at first,
lost in the moment
among my friends

I have spent every moment of my life
since I was eight,
listening for the call,
praying to the silence,
and lying in wait

But now when it comes,
I am distracted instead,

And when I notice it–
when I answer,
the voice sounds
distant and deep,
as though from far off,
calling from somewhere
in the darkness of sleep.

The dream has come calling.

*They want to publish the book.*

## Twenty-Eight

I wish I'd known all this ten years ago,
but here it is, some words for younger me:

I wish you could see how much I've grown
and everything I've accomplished
in these years on my own.

I wish you could see everything I've overcome,
the troubles I faced on the hardest days –
you would be proud of the person I've become.

I know you always had such
high expectations of who I could be
and I did my best,
but I'm sorry it took me so long to see,
to be grateful for all that you did –
to be grateful for all of *me*.

I turned twenty-eight today,
and I don't know what tomorrow brings,
but I made it here, after so many years.
I know it sounds silly to celebrate,
but there were a lot of hard nights
and a whole ocean of tears.

I don't spend enough time
appreciating the things I've done.
So please, while you're young,
look back at yourself
and be proud of who you have become.

I am so grateful to be here,

To be happy and healthy,
to share all my stories with whoever will listen,
to have things to look forward to each day,
to have a roof over my head,
warm food filling my belly,
and enough money
that I don't have to struggle
to live comfortably.

I want this for *you*,
and if you're reading this –
maybe it's all you *really* want too.

Just know,
when you're down so dark in the deep
and you can't see the surface above,
there is a light waiting for you,
a new shore up here.

And you'll find it one day,
if you're fortunate and patient enough.

So don't you dare let go,
don't give up,
not when the storm comes
and the journey gets rough.

Here we are at the end,
and yet, the end is just another beginning –
another chance to *begin* again.

# Acknowledgments

Gregory B., I love you more than you'll ever know. Thank you for all the talks, the hugs, the tears, the laughs, and the lessons. I've been profoundly shaped by your guidance, love, and wisdom.

Christie – Beautiful Queen – you are so incredibly special to me. Through you, I've learned so much about life, love, and family. You are the source of so many of my talents and abilities and strength.

Shannon, if it wasn't for you, I don't know who I would be today. You gave me the freedom, trust, and support to explore myself and the world in ways no one else did, and it's one of the most valuable gifts I've ever had.

Sue and Ron, thank you for being a constant through the ups and downs in life. Your reliability and love shown through your actions speaks volumes.

Caitlin, you truly are my other half. Your constant bravery, optimism, and strength have been an inspiration to me since the very beginning.

Karissa, you always make me feel like I'm not alone in life. Our similar trajectories and your never-ending humor and love give me a sense of peace that can't be undervalued.

Brittany, your consistent friendship is a rock for me. You've always been a role model and someone I admire. It's been so fun to grow up alongside you.

Leeza, your warmth, sincerity, and generosity is incomparable. I am grateful every day I get to talk to you. You're such a bright light in my life and are always an inspiration.

Brandon, you're the best little brother. I love the friendship we have and the memories we've made growing up together. You're an amazing example of strength, growth, and capability.

Carli, you're a powerhouse of encouragement, love, and positivity. You help me see the world from different perspectives, and I'm forever grateful that I get to call you my sister.

Justin Estcourt, your artwork is always beautiful and your patience with us is much appreciated. Thank you for your talent, creativity, and time.

Thank you to our wonderful team of people at Andrews McMeel Publishing – Patty, Danys, Riley, we appreciate all the hard work you do to help make this book great. James, thank you for your belief in us.

Thank you to you, our readers. We are so incredibly grateful to you. Not a day goes by that we take you for granted.

Did you enjoy reading our story?

It continues in our second book, *Maybe Today*, and then in our first book, *Love by Night*.

Check both out if you want to read more about us and where our lives went after this story.

You can find more of our words on
Instagram and TikTok @skwilliamspoetry.

Please feel free to write to us!

Andrews McMeel Publishing

a division of Andrews McMeel Universal

1130 Walnut Street, Kansas City, Missouri 64106

www.andrewsmcmeel.com

24 25 26 27 28 TEN 10 9 8 7 6 5 4 3 2 1

ISBN: 978-1-5248-7736-1

Library of Congress Control Number: 2023948111

Cover Art and Design by Justin Estcourt

Editor: Patty Rice
Designer: Julie Barnes
Production Editor: Dave Shaw
Production Manager: Shona Burns